First American Edition, 2011

Published in the United States
Copyright © 2009-2012 Ronald S. Phillips

All Rights reserved under International and Pan-American Copyright Conventions. No part of this publication may be reproduced, stored in a retrieval system, or transmitted in any form or by any means, electronic, mechanical, photo-copying, recording, or otherwise, without the prior written permission of the copyright owner.

This book is written for educational purposes only. IT IS NOT INTENDED AS FINANCIAL, TAX OR LEGAL ADVICE. For specific financial, tax and legal questions please consult with an appropriately licensed professional. All examples and illustrations are for illustrative purposes only and are not recommendations for specific investments or asset classes. Investments in the financial markets are not FDIC insured or bank guaranteed and you may lose your principal. The author and publisher specifically disclaim any liability that is incurred from the application or use of the contents of this book.

VOLUME ONE

The Armchair Investment Reader

FEATURING exclusive article reprints from a licensed financial advisor & trusted financial columnist

Ronald S. Phillips
Independent Financial Advisor

SPECIAL THANKS TO

Jim Grasso, publisher
Senior Beacon Newspaper

CONTENTS

Introduction..11

State of the Stimulus.......................................17
Will China Rule the World?..............................20
USA on Sale..23
A Near-Perfect Investment?..............................26
How to Stretch Your IRA.................................29
Five Sure-Fire Ways to Conquer Inflation............32
Dealing with Dollars' Dismal Decline..................35
Asset Allocation is Dead…(Or is It?)...................38
Vaccinate Against the Gold Bug.........................41
How to Minimize Your
Estate Taxes While Keeping Your Sanity..............44
Market Re-Cap for the Decade..........................47
What's an Investor to Do?.................................50
Live Like a Rockefeller for $5,000......................53
Correction Knocks Market................................56
How to Pick a Mutual Fund..............................59
Don't Dread Deflation.....................................62
Making the Grade..65
How to Pick a Financial Advisor........................69
GM Makes a Comeback..................................72
Finally Bullish...75
5 Investor Moves for the New Year....................79

Australia: Gateway to Asia Riches?......................................83
Two Ways to Pick a Stock....................................…...86
One-Time Rodney Dangerfield of
Investments Now Industry Behemoth......................89
How to Lower Your Gold Risk..............................…...93
The 3-Step No-Brainer
Mutual Fund Strategy...…..96
How to Avoid Bad Information............................…..99
"We the Debtors…of the United States
of America"……………………………………………………..102
The #1 Investing Technique..............................…105
Ten Biggest Investor Mistakes: Part 1...................…...108
Ten Biggest Investor Mistakes: Part 2...................…...111

Quotes……………………………………………....……117

About The Author…………………………………………123

The Most Implausible FREE Gift Ever……....……..…124

INTRODUCTION

It has been an eventful time. The world, and the U.S. in particular, have experienced truly historic events. We hear it all the time, "This time is different." Well, it **really has** been different these last few years, and the last decade.

Consider these examples:

- From 2000-2002 the S&P 500 experienced three down years in a row—which only happens about every forty years
- Then the unthinkable occurred: the S&P 500 performance was negative for the last **decade**. An investor putting in $10,000 at the end of 1999 ended up with just $9,090 a decade later—which has not happened once in the last 200 years!
- Treasury bonds outperformed stocks for a three-decade period—the first time since **before** The Civil War!
- The unemployment rate has been above 8% for more

than 31 straight months—the longest "streak" since records have been kept
- Gold has had its best performance in 90 years—notching 11 years of positive gains!
- Topping these events was the downgrade of the United States credit rating—this has never happened in the history of the U.S., either!

Whew! That is a lot of exclamation points. Fortunately, even volatile times return to normal. Eventually. And, the more extreme, usually the **better** the rebound on the way up.

A BRIGHT FUTURE

It is hard to drive a car using the rear view mirrors. We have to use the front windshield and look to the horizon of the future. The American economy has a bright one, indeed.

The U.S. economy has the most diverse industries and sectors of any country, past and present. We have a retail sector nearly as big as China's **entire** economy and a manufacturing sector nearly as big. We also have roughly five times more gross production than the "Rising Dragon." This is the largest output of any country currently and for years to come.

POPULATION WOES

Many nations are facing population shortages in the future. Russia, Japan, Germany, Italy, South Korea, even China, are *all* estimated to have smaller populations, by the year 2050. This is not a good thing for those economies. Yet, the U.S. is estimated to have steady, healthy population increases.

Speaking of populations, America has the largest, most vibrant, immigrant population of any country on the planet. Why is that good? Many of our new innovations and advances are imagined and implemented by the over 38,000,000 vibrant immigrants living here. This accounts for more than 20% of the world's immigrant population. This "new blood" has contributed to the strength and growth of the U.S. since before our country was created.

INNOVATIVE PROSPECTS

Mining asteroids. Private-sector space flights sending civilians into orbit. In-home healthcare robots. The two-year-shelf-life sandwich. 3-D printers churning out customizable bones. Driverless cars. Laser headlights. Sewage-powered cars (jokes coming soon). All of these ideas are being worked on mainly by American universities and companies. *That* is innovation. And that is just the beginning of the dynamism of the United States.

The U.S. also has an incredibly advanced political engine. We still broker most of the major pacts between disagreeing nations, adding to our political capital and economic capital.

I believe we will all look back five years from now and say, "What a bargain the U.S. was! I wish I had invested more at those cheap prices." Only time will tell, but I will place my bets on the most dynamic and resilient economy ever built.

* * *

I hope you get some insight from these articles. Also, take them with a grain of salt. They are timely and can be taken out of context as the investment landscape changes.

Some of the articles are bold and opinionated. Some are general. Some offer step-by-step instructions. Some, hopefully, will stand the test of time. Thank you very much for taking *your* time to read this book!

Ronald S. Phillips
Independent Financial Advisor

STATE OF THE STIMULUS

Let me make one thing clear. Any economic stimulus will help the nation recover from this recession (and help avoid bigger problems). Sending out money into the economy and spending on anything will make money flow and circulate. I've heard reports that the current plan could add anywhere from 2.5 to 4% to our economic growth. Any of those numbers would be a great thing. But are we going about it in the right way? Could we improve it? Or enhance it? Definitely.

Let's take a look at the recent examples of our smart, Asian friends across the pond. According to a recent *Business Week* article, there are four major countries turning out their own brand of stimulus. Taiwan, China, Thailand and Japan are currently, or are very close to, sending out billions of dollars of government money.

They are all using the same method: vouchers that can be used like cash and have an expiration date. For example, Taiwan is sending out a $108 voucher to **every one of its 23 million citizens.** The voucher must be spent by yearend. Several major cities in China are sending out thirty dollars. Thailand is sending out 10 million checks worth $58. Lastly, Japan will be sending anywhere from $130-200 to every citizen.

Of course, all of these countries and cities have a much smaller population than the United States. So this type of stimulus, even for roughly 100 million citizens in Japan, will only cost $20 billion at the high end. Although if you put the recent $800 billion stimulus into perspective that would be quite a voucher. The government could send a check to every U.S. home for $1000 every three months for the next year and spend half of the recent stimulus amount. This would have a far-reaching result in many areas of the economy, lighten some of the burden of the recession on the middle class *and* increase our GDP. It would also be democratic, too, reaching every household in America.

Where would all of this money end up? Admittedly it would be concentrated into the retail sector. It would also be spread throughout utility companies, discounters and other industries. But it would rotate money throughout our country. If we make the vouchers expire in six to twelve months then we also ensure a *consistent* increase in the economy.

Another plus of a program like this is the flexibility of the vouchers. If the economy rebounds in three quarters we could stop the last voucher from ever leaving the mail. If we need more stimulus then we could extend the vouchers for another quarter or another year if need be.

What would you rather do…send billions to the banks or spend a little of the governments' (our) money?

Originally published in April, 2009.

WILL CHINA RULE THE WORLD?

It seems like everywhere you turn there is a new article, study or TV special about how China is going to dominate the world economy. And, yes, they are the fastest-growing economy for the past 20 years (they have averaged about 9-10% annually over this time). They have even recently surpassed Germany as the *third-largest* economy (although they are essentially tied for size in 2007).

Yet, we need to put this very enviable growth into perspective. The bottom line is that they simply have A LOT more mouths to feed. Consider that:

- By the year 2050 China is projected to have almost *1.5 billion people*

- <u>*Per person*</u>, their gross domestic product (GDP) is still very small (see examples below) and

- Is 9% even a sustainable growth rate for China (possibly but *probably* not)?

(Statistics: Wikipedia)

Seeing as Germany has been ousted to fourth place world-wide let's take a closer look at their numbers. They have been the number three economy for years and it weighs in at $3.3 trillion. They have a relatively small population of about 83 million people. Some simple division brings their GDP per person to $40,400. That is very significant when compared to China's per-person GDP of only $2,483. In other words, China has successfully created the third largest economy in the world. But they still have a fairly low average standard of living (although that is rapidly going up, too).

How does all of this fare for the U.S.? Take a look at the figures in the box and you will see that the U.S. has a per-person GDP that is about **eighteen times larger** than that of China. You will also see that tiny Luxembourg is the wealthiest by this measure. Of course, they have the opposite position of China. Their population is just a blip, barely the size of Pueblo, CO and Colorado Springs, CO combined.

> GROSS DOMESTIC PRODUCT PER CITIZEN& RANK:
>
> Luxembourg (#1)--$103,125
> United States (#12)--$45,725
> Germany (#19)--$40,400
> China (#107)--$2,483
>
> (Source: International Monetary Fund)

If we projected growth of the U.S. at just 3% annually and China at 9% annually until the year 2050 we would continue to have a wealthier population at that time. The United States would average over $121,000 and China's average would be slightly over $50,000 per citizen (although in terms of total size we would be second). That still brings into question if a nation can *sustain* a nine percent growth rate for over sixty years. And we can grow **over three percent** domestically if we put our minds to it (see last month's article about investing into renewable energy for specifics).

So will China be a fierce competitor and eventually have a larger total economy than the U.S. and many other Western and Asian countries? Probably. On per-person income and GDP do they have many, many years (and even decades) to reach the high levels of the U.S. and other developed regions? Probably. Will China be a political and military threat in the future? Or are they right now? I will *gladly* leave those questions to a current affairs columnist....

Originally published in May, 2009.

USA...ON SALE

The U.S. is the largest, most-diverse economy on the planet. We make, grow and service just about anything you can imagine. We are also, ethnically and religiously, the most-diverse nation in history.

Because of these factors we have a resilient and consistent economy. U.S. government debt is the only investment that I, as a financial advisor, can legally call risk-free. That is because we have never defaulted on our national debt instruments.

Those debts could be one of our largest current problems. Are we getting too deep in debt? Most people would say yes. In general, I agree with that. We need to bring these levels down. We are the biggest debtor in the world in dollar terms. But we should look at our debt as a *percent of GDP*. When measured that way we are inline with several Western European nations and Japan (source: Wikipedia.com).

We also need this "deficit spending" when we are

in tough economic periods. Government spending will help to float the economy to better times (and avoid even worse times).

Although the U.S. *does* need to safeguard our pristine, AAA credit rating. Just as I'm writing this Great Britain is losing their AAA rating. This will raise their interest costs and lower the desirability of their bonds. We need to protect this valuable asset of ours.

Where's the silver lining?

Despite the recent market run-up stocks are still very cheap. The Dow Jones Industrial Average (DJIA) is down an average of 0.61% over the last ten years (source: Dow Jones). This is essentially flat since 1998. So, in other words, we can pick up thirty large, multinational stocks for the same price as a decade ago.

Yet at that time the economy was only at $9.2 trillion. Today it is roughly $13 trillion. That is forty-one percent growth and we can buy at a ten-year discount. How often do prices drop to those levels for an even stronger asset?

There are several ways to play the U.S. market. You can buy all of the actual components in the DJIA. It is called the **Dow Diamonds** (symbol: **DIA**). The price is about $1\text{-}100^{th}$ the value of the Dow. It's about $82.78 today and has a very respectable yield of 3.57 percent.

If you want something with more than thirty stocks and representative of the whole market take a look at

iShares Dow Jones U.S. Total Market (symbol: **IYY**). This index fund owns about 95% of the entire U.S. stock market, including stocks of all sizes and valuations. Another similar broad-market index fund is the **iShares Russell 3000** (symbol: **IWV**). This fund includes about 86% of the U.S. stocks traded.

With solid population growth and consistent economic growth I would bet, along with Warren Buffett, on the U.S. for the long haul.

Originally published in June, 2009.

A Near-Perfect Investment?

Of course there is no absolutely ideal investment. There are investments that are too risky, don't pay any income, don't keep up with inflation, are not liquid or are too volatile.

But what if, at the right time in the market, you could find a *near-perfect* asset? One that currently has an annual income roughly double the yield of 30-year treasury bonds, has risk that is less than half the S&P 500 index, is liquid and outpaces inflation, is federally tax-exempt *and* Warren Buffett just endorsed by buying gobs of?

You may have already guessed what this unique investment is. It's a bond type I have been writing about in my newsletter and talking to clients about for well over a year. It is **municipal bonds**.

Municipal bonds are local government bonds that are obligations of a city or some project in that city. For example, there are E-470 toll-road bonds. Those bonds pay interest from the revenue raised from the tolls. Or you could have a "general obligation" bond for Colorado that goes to some kind of general expense. These "G.O." bonds are backed fully by those respective states' revenues and ability to pay.

CURRENTLY OUTPACING INFLATION

With "munis" you can get a little bit of capital appreciation (or depreciation) but the main return is from the income. Currently the income from many "muni funds" is significantly higher than the average 3-5% rate of inflation. Just the other day a client of mine went into one of these funds and is receiving an eight percent annual yield.

Municipal bonds also have about half of the risk of the stock market. They are backed by local governments which usually have debt limitations. They are also, unlike stocks, obligated to pay interest to the investors. This all adds up to less volatility and more safety.

TAX-EXEMPT INCOME

With tax-deferred investing you *eventually* pay taxes. Tax-exempt income goes one step better. You could receive a monthly check from your municipal bond fund and not pay any federal taxes at all. If the bonds are located in your home state you also avoid state taxes. [Please check with your tax expert for further details regarding your personal tax situation].

Let's compare tax-exempt muni income to the after-tax return of the stock market. Say an investor is in the 25% tax bracket and they get a *taxable* return of 10.5% for the year (the historic stock return average). After taxes they would pocket 7.87 percent. Remember that some quality municipal bond funds are yielding a little over 8% annually.

STILL UNDER-VALUED AND HIGH-YIELDING

Municipal bonds are still a good value when compared to similar Treasury bonds. In a normal interest-rate environment a 30-year T-bond should yield higher than a 30-year muni bond. Currently the opposite is true and could make now a good time to investigate these "near-perfect" investments.

Originally published in August, 2009.

HOW TO STRETCH YOUR IRA

We work long and hard. We save money for a rainy day. If we are really savvy we invest in tax-deferred accounts like IRAs (Individual Retirement Accounts), a 401k or annuities. Then we reach that "sudden stop at the end". And our offspring get to enrich the government with even more tax dollars. Or do they?

Is there a way around paying the government a big lump-sum payment when we pass along retirement accounts to our loved ones? Fortunately, there is a way. It's called "stretching" your IRA.

Let's assume you have already set up an IRA. Or you have retired from a job or business and then converted your 401k into an IRA. This technique can help your heirs *slowly* pay taxes to the government. The key word is *slowly*. There are very, very few ways of *completely* avoiding all taxes.

Without this technique your heirs would receive a big lump of cash when you pass away. *Then* they would be forced to pay a big lump to the government. If they were in the 15% federal bracket and the IRA amount is high enough they could be bumped up into the 25% bracket. Add in state tax and the total tax rate could be nearly thirty percent *or more*.

The stretch technique does just what it sounds like. For example, if your son or daughter is 35 when they receive your IRA this could put *their* remaining life expectancy at 46.2 years. This figure is important. Your beneficiary would divide the balance of the IRA by 46.2 (or whatever real figure it is) and must take a small distribution based on that number.

If the balance happened to be $92,400 then it would equal a distribution of $2000 **instead** of the total account value. [That is 92,400 divided by 46.2 = 2000] Each year the figure would change but the idea is the same. They avoided the lump-sum tax and possibly being in a higher bracket. Now they are only taxed on the $2000 distribution that year. Pretty sneaky isn't it?

Of course, the main benefit is forty-six more years of tax-deferred growth on the underlying assets. Tax-deferral is usually always a good thing because any gains grow quicker without the burden of annual taxes.

Keep in mind that my example is a simplification of this technique. You should always check with your tax professional for all details regarding your specific situation.

Also, remember to name your beneficiaries on your accounts. When you do that you should be able to take advantage of this technique. If you do not put down a specific beneficiary then it could default to your estate and you get no stretch option.

Originally published in September, 2009.

5 Sure-Fire Ways to Conquer Inflation

In the last few quarters America has had *deflation*. We have been reeling from a tsunami-like financial meltdown. That has, in turn, popped the inflation bubble for the time being. Everyone around the globe is buying and using less "stuff" so inflation is in check. So what do we have to worry about it for?

Under normal circumstances the government has a policy of "encouraging" moderate inflation in the 3-5 percent annual range. Also, the government is printing a lot of money which could *potentially* heat up inflation.

So we always want to be ready to fight that specter of rising costs. Here are five ways to do that. Two are active investments. They take more time and expertise. The other three are passive and therefore easier to manage and maintain (music to my ears…and probably yours, too).

THE TWO ACTIVE WAYS TO CONQUER INFLATION

Real estate is a wonderful way to outpace rising expenses. Assuming you have property that has a positive cash flow you should do fine over time. The income is the main return, for example, a 7% cash flow. Then add in 3-5% annual appreciation and you have defeated inflation.

Then we have **business ownership**. Let's say you sell widgets and make a 10% net profit. Then your costs go up. Now you raise the costs to your customers. You have effectively knocked out inflation again.

These are, of course, oversimplifications. As I said before, there is a lot of management and time involved with both real estate and business ownership.

THE THREE PASSIVE WAYS TO CONQUER INFLATION

My favorite ways to overcome inflation are the simplest. Keep doing what you are doing to earn income. Then invest into one or all of these areas.

The first vehicle is **the stock market**. Over the course of more than eight decades stocks have been the best way to passively beat both inflation *and* taxes. The historic return is over 10% annually. Even during The Great Depression and the current Great Recession the market has been the place to be.

The second vehicle is the **municipal bond market**. I don't mention the other bond markets because municipals have that magic ingredient: tax advantage. They are federally tax-exempt and sometimes state tax-exempt. That makes them a little bit more powerful that even a Treasury bond or corporate bond.

The last tool in our belt is so obvious you may not have even thought of it. **Save more**. If the excesses of the past decade have taught us anything I hope it is to save more. Remember, just a year or two ago the U.S. had a negative savings rate. Then it was barely a fraction of a percent. So combat inflation by saving 3-5 percent more and then invest that into the other four areas.

Let's say you have a $100,000 income and now you are saving an additional $3-5 thousand annually. You are setting aside the rate of inflation and now this money is compounding, furthering your fight against this soon-to-be raging beast called inflation.

Originally published in October, 2009.

DEALING WITH DOLLARS' DISMAL DECLINE

You have seen the headlines of trillion-dollar budget deficits. You have seen the headlines of U.S. trade deficits. Lately you have also seen the headlines of the drop in the actual value of the dollar. The more-urgent figure is the $1.4 trillion budget deficit. The higher this number is the weaker our dollar tends to be. This high number lowers confidence in our ability to repay our debts.

We have gotten out of this mess before and we will do it again…eventually. According to Wikipedia, in the late 1940s our debt as a percent of GDP was over 110 percent. And it looks like we are rapidly heading there again. As of 2008 we were at 70.2 percent. The end of 2009 public debt is estimated to be 90.4 percent of GDP. "The more things change the more they stay the same."

In the meantime, it could be helpful to have some strategies to combat this weakening dollar problem. There are actually quite a few "bullets" to choose from.

The most-effective could be to invest in currencies other than the U.S. dollar. This is readily available to investors of even modest net worth. There are new mutual funds that invest in euros, the Australian dollar and even a basket of different currencies. The "gold standard" currency is considered the Swiss franc. The Swiss tend to have a healthy government balance sheet and want to maintain that as "the world's bankers." They pay very low interest but it can be made up by appreciation in the value of the franc.

Another method to fight the dollars' weakness is foreign government bonds that are denominated in those foreign currencies. The easiest way to do this is to buy a mutual fund that handles all of the management. You can get higher yields than simply holding a different currency. There are also other risks like maturity dates and possible foreign defaults on debt.

My last method of "currency insurance" is simply to buy U.S. TIPs (Treasury Inflation Protected securities). These are U.S. government bonds that pay a base-rate and also the rate of inflation. Currently they are low-yielding but they could increase yields for two reasons. Interest rates are so low that future rates are probably only headed up. And a weakening dollar is essentially the *inflating* of that currency. So these bonds would pay higher yields if high inflation/weak dollar scenarios play out.

Again, we have been here before and gotten out of it. We can do it again. The U.S. government is still considered the safest investment risk available. Also, we have the largest gross output of any nation (over $23 trillion) and we continue to grow. Now, can we just shrink our deficit?

Originally published in November, 2009.

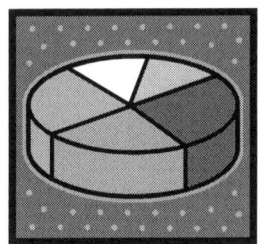

ASSET ALLOCATION IS DEAD... (OR IS IT?)

That is what I have heard lately. I read a lot of investing industry magazines and I have run across quite a few headlines declaring asset allocation dead. You may have seen some yourself. It makes for a sensational headline but I have to disagree on this short-sightedness. Fortunately, some things really do last the test of time. And this strategy is one of them. It was even promoted by Warren Buffett's mentor Ben Graham.

As a reminder, asset allocation is the process of determining your risk tolerance and crafting a portfolio of unique asset classes that work together to provide upside return and minimize downside risk. The goal is to capture <u>most</u> of the stock and bond market return while holding onto <u>more</u> of your principal during major market meltdowns.

The key benefit of asset allocation is MINIMIZING RISK. And in practice it does actually work. For example, a growth-oriented client of mine was down in value by about 24 percent during the big drop earlier this year (he was fully asset allocated into more than a dozen unique categories and investment styles). Well, that's nothing to be proud of. I don't want any clients' accounts down even a fraction of a percent. But we have to look at the performance relative to a benchmark. The S&P 500 was down about 48% during this same time. So if your neighbor was fully invested in the S&P and you had this asset allocation you "outperformed" her by over 20 percent.

In dollar terms $100,000 would have turned into about $76,000. Your neighbor's hundred thousand would have been $52,000. Right away we can see the benefit of losing less...*minimizing risk*. Also, your higher account value has less of a struggle back up. If your more-conservative portfolio went up only 30 percent you would have $98,800. If the S&P 500 investor went up 45 percent they would still be below your value during the decline: $75,400.

So how do you create an asset allocation?

The first step is to figure out your risk tolerance. In my book there is an entire chapter on this strategy along with five questions that can guide you toward a specific allocation (along with percentages and pie charts). You can also find dozens of these questionnaires on the internet. Do a Google search for "asset allocation questionnaire" and you will find many good ones from **Money-Zine.com**, **SmartMoney.com, Yahoo.com** and others.

The next step is to see what percentages are recommended for the various asset classes. It may range from a few percent to over 15 percent into certain assets. Some of the investments may be different-sized stocks, different styles of stocks, U.S. corporate bonds, government bonds, international stocks and bonds, commodities, cash, foreign currencies, "short" investments and more. These allocations assume a certain amount of investing knowledge.

Next you simply invest as recommended or tweak it to your liking. Here's to a prosperous new year and to minimized risk.

Originally published in December, 2009.

VACCINATE AGAINST THE GOLD BUG

I don't know if your TV remote has the button that lets you switch back and forth between two channels. But I was doing that one evening and could almost see a bubble forming on my TV. I was switching back and forth between two "Buy gold" or "We'll buy your gold" commercials. They're everywhere! You can hear it on the radio, on television, magazines, newspapers, in the mail… everywhere. When I go outside I look up at the sky and half-expect to see an airplane with a banner proclaiming "Buy gold!"

If there was ever a bubble I think this is it. I was convinced when I heard the nation of India bought 200 <u>tons</u> of gold for their reserves *and* are set to get another 200 tons of gold.

Can you still make money on gold and other precious metals? Sure you can. But the big question is when will the ride stop? Will gold investors be stuck in a decade of flat performance like in the past?

If possible I like to us the Buffett Litmus Test for investing trends. Is Warren Buffett investing in this sector? What did Warren do during the Tech Boom (and Bubble)? He waited on the sidelines and actually got criticized for "missing" the new era. What is Warren doing with gold and precious metals? I'm not completely sure but about five years ago he did invest over $100 million in silver at a little over five dollars per ounce. These were historically low prices not seen in 20 years. I haven't heard about Buffett buying gold by the ton yet.

But isn't gold an inflation hedge? Yes and no. At times it appears that gold prices move with inflation. But if you look at an historic price chart for gold it doesn't really move evenly with inflation. A truer inflation hedge in the past has been real estate. Real estate is a tangible asset that we live in. And inflation is the price of tangible goods going up. I consider gold a "doomsday" asset that people rush to in tough times.

Aren't there a lot of industrial and commercial uses for gold? There are a lot of miscellaneous uses. But they don't add up to much demand. The main use is in jewelry. Now people are spending much less on those discretionary items. Oil, on the other hand, has constant and growing demand and may deserve to be at high price levels.

So I applaud everyone who has made money in precious metals. But just remember the lessons from the Tech Bubble. What goes irrationally up must come down.

Originally published in January, 2010.

How to Minimize Your Estate Taxes While Keeping Your Sanity

It's official. The year to die is 2010. This year the estate tax is zero. You could have $20 million and not pay a dime of estate taxes if your "will expired" in 2010.

What will the estate tax be next year? According to *RetireIQ.com*, the 2011 estate tax exemption will be $1 million. Any assets you might leave *over* that exemption will have a flat 55% tax generously given to the government…the dreaded "death tax."

There are several strategies to potentially minimize your estate and to make it easier to pay for the tax. Below are several general suggestions. Please always verify any ideas with licensed CPAs, attorneys and financial advisors. Some actions you take could be irrevocable.

IDEA #1: GIFTING

This is a very common idea but I have some unique takes on this one.

You can give away $13,000 to any person annually and that person does not have to pay gift taxes. We just minimized your estate *and* avoided gift tax. If you are married you can bump that up to $26,000 a year.

Where this gets interesting is when you use a tax-deferred 529 college savings plan. These newer plans offer an accelerated five-year contribution. For example, if a married couple has a grandchild they want to fund college expenses for, this can add up quickly. They could put $130,000 ($26,000 times five years) into a 529 plan with a single contribution. If they had 3 grandchildren they could give up to $390,000, moving it out of their estate. Sorry Uncle Sam.

Another gifting strategy is giving the $13,000 in the form of a zero-coupon bond. This adds predetermined growth to the gift. For example, a $25,000 (face-value) zero-coupon bond might only cost $13,000. When the bond matures it will pay the $25,000 face-value. So you have effectively given the $13,000 *plus* the future growth, eliminating any additional build-up in your estate.

IDEA #2: DIRECT PAYMENTS

Another idea that is very similar to gifting is directly paying for a person's medical bills and/or their school tuition. According to *FinWeb.com*, this person does not even have to be a relative. Any amount for these two expenses is allowed. But it must be paid directly to the provider. Then the gift is out of the givers' taxable estate.

IDEA #3: BUY LIFE INSURANCE

You can use life insurance proceeds as a way to help your loved ones pay a future estate tax bill. For example, a seventy-year old man believes he will have a taxable estate of $1 million in the future. At the current 55% tax rate his bill would be $550,000.

He buys a twenty-year, $500,000 term-life policy that costs $10,000 annually. Let's say he dies at age ninety. He paid roughly $200,000 over the life of the policy (more funds out of his estate) and now his family has $500,000 to offset the estimated estate tax. Voila…his taxes are taken care of. Better luck next time Uncle Sam.

Originally published in March, 2010.

MARKET RE-CAP FOR THE DECADE

What a ride we have all experienced in the past ten years!

Of course, the biggest news of the decade is the performance of the S&P 500 index. In a rare event the index actually experienced a decade-long decline. If you had invested $10,000 on the last day of 1999 you would have $9,090 at the beginning of this year (*source: Bloomberg.com*). *The Wall Street Journal* went so far as to say that is the worst 10-year performance in two centuries.

How did the other asset classes do? Gold had a stellar 15% average annual return. Bonds gave a respectable 6.33% average and home prices returned 4.74% (*source: Standard & Poor's*).

Is this really the death of U.S. equities?

Short answer: no. Long answer: all of the fundamentals are in place for stock market gains. The U.S. economy at the end of 1999 was about $9.1 trillion and at the end of 2009 is estimated to be $14.2 trillion, showing significant growth. Interest rates are near 95-year lows. Experts have said that is good for the stock market. The federal debt and trade deficit are actually within historic ranges as a percentage of our overall economy.

This can all add up to market growth...at least it should. We have had decades and longer periods of flat stock markets.

What is an investor to do or not do? A key thing to *avoid* is chasing after the previous market leaders. No one knows which asset class will continue to do well or will sink to the bottom of the pile this year. Also, focus on income from assets. For stocks make sure there is a healthy dividend. You can include bonds and other income types for diversification and steady interest.

This approach is called asset allocation. Own a little "chunk" of many unique asset types like bonds, foreign bonds, commodities, U.S. stocks, international stocks, small and large companies and other distinct investments.

Asset allocation throughout the last decade has done better than the stock market index. A basic allocation with 40% bonds, 50% assorted stocks, 5% real estate and 5% commodities had an average return of 5.4 percent per year. This was achieved with less risk than the stock market and significantly less risk than individual assets like gold and emerging markets. So in an emergency you have a greater chance of having your principal than in riskier assets. Also, this approach lets you capture a lot of the upside of the stock market when it does outperform.

So while we had a very eventful decade the next ten years could provide solid returns for stocks. It can even provide solid returns without the market melodrama if we stick to a smart allocation approach.

Originally published in April, 2010.

What's an Investor to Do?

The economy is improving, jobs are stabilizing, stock & bond markets have rebounded significantly...all great news. But there remain several surprises in Pandora's Box. One that can have a major impact on ordinary folks is interest rates.

Wait. Aren't rates at historic lows?

They are and that is the problem. They are actually at momentous, 95-plus year lows. The federal interest rate has never been lower.

What happens when rates rise? And how can we prepare our investments for that eventuality?

Unlike most of the economic hype out there rising rates do matter to most people. Rising rates can have a domino effect, influencing many areas of our lives. Of course, some peoples' mortgage and other loan payments go up. Investors can collect more interest from CDs, bonds and other fixed income securities. Stock and bond values can go haywire (meaning increased volatility and possibly declining values). With stocks up over fifty percent they are due for a correction. Rates going up could be the catalyst.

So what can an investor do?

There are several ways to fight this beast. One thing to do within your fixed income investments is to lower the overall maturity dates. For example, if you were looking at a one-year or a five-year CD you may want to opt for the shorter term. This allows you to capture the higher rates of future certificates

This lower maturity strategy can be used for bonds and bond funds, too. If you have mutual funds you can go to *Morningstar.com* and figure out the average maturity of your underlying bonds for free. The site will categorize your fund as short, intermediate or long term. Also, it will show an average duration and maybe even an average maturity. This is important because you want the shorter terms now. I am currently recommending funds as short as 2-3 months. These should do well with rising interest. This also lowers bond volatility because long-term bonds can drop in value as rates rise.

Another strategy is to make sure you are invested into quality investments. The reason why is because even if we have a correction (drop) in the markets you will want to hang on. These drops can be very quick and you don't want to mistime the market and then lose on future gains.

Because corporate profits are up, GDP is growing and other good fundamentals we should see a general rise in the markets. I don't think we will have a repeat of the "lost decade" we just went through. So hanging on really is the best advice this time around.

Originally published in May, 2010.

LIVE LIKE A ROCKEFELLER FOR $5,000

I have to apologize for the headline. I didn't find any cheap mansions or yachts or hidden-away European villas for that price. What I did discover was a way we can imitate the <u>generosity</u> of the Rockefellers. The family contributed to just about any cause you could think of, including higher education, health & medicine, national parks and other causes.

It's an American tradition to be generous. According to Giving USA Foundation, Americans gave $307 billion to charitable causes in 2008. As reported by the World Bank, the U.S. is also the largest giver as a percent of GDP than any other country in the world.

How did the famous Rockefeller family structure their gifts? Mainly through foundations that perpetuate giving and grow with markets…to further perpetuate giving. But how do ordinary folks accomplish that without the high-maintenance, high asset requirements and high costs of a private foundation? Use a donor advised fund (DAF).

Donor Advised Funds are like Quasi-Foundations

They have very similar characteristics and are more private, easier to maintain and are easier to start than a foundation. Like the headline suggests the asset minimums start at just five thousand dollars although some funds require ten thousand dollars. Total management and administration expenses are relatively small, ranging from 0.15% up to about 1.8% annually. The differences are determined by which companies manage the account and how much in assets are contributed.

There are many large financial companies that assist in these accounts. Some are Fidelity, Vanguard, T. Rowe Price and Eaton Vance. All of these companies have no set-up fees. They are all "one-stop shops," offering a complete suite of services. They provide the administrative oversight, trust duties *and* investment management.

What's in it For the Giver?

According to Eaton Vance the donor advised funds allow you to:

- Be eligible for an immediate tax deduction

- Avoid capital gains on appreciated securities used for funding the account
- Avoid estate taxes and
- Create a legacy of giving

For example, if a couple were to set up a DAF they could contribute their $10,000 worth of appreciated stock that they purchased for $3,000. They would avoid the capital gains tax on the seven thousand dollar increase and get the money out of their estate. At the 15% gains rate they would have saved $1,050 in taxes. They can now direct the fund to make grants of as little as $50 to the tax-exempt charities of their choice.

These are all very significant benefits in addition to the joy the giver gets from helping their favorite charities. As always, check with your tax preparer or accountant for specific tax implications for your situation.

Originally published in June, 2010.

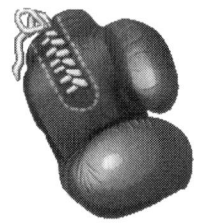

Correction Knocks Market

The stock market has just experienced its latest correction. This is very common and should have been expected. The reason why is because the Dow Jones Industrial Average had gained about 69 percent from its market lows in March, 2009. After a strong run-up like that we often see weakness in stocks. I warned about a correction in mid-April for that exact reason.

> **Correction:**
> "A reverse movement, usually negative, of at least 10% in a stock, bond, commodity or index. Corrections are generally temporary price declines, interrupting an uptrend in the market or asset."
>
> Source: Investopedia.com

Is This the Beginning of a Bear?

No one really knows what this could mean. The fundamentals of the economy are rapidly improving despite some major negatives like government debt and high unemployment. The U.S. economy is estimated to hit $15 _trillion_ for the first time in history this year. Our diverse industries are creating a stable recovery. Also, unemployment should drop by roughly one percent each year as we continue to grow.

How to Take Advantage of This Drop

Like the definition says corrections are typically temporary and part of an uptrend. That is good news. We can use this as a time to buy cheaper.

There are several ways to "play" this opportunity. I always recommend using mutual funds for the diversity and avoidance of catastrophic loss as compared to an individual stock or bond. One version is an exchange-traded fund.

Two that stand out are **SPDR Dow Jones Industrial Average ETF** (symbol: DIA) and **iShares Dow Jones U.S. Total Stock Market Index** (symbol: IWV).

DIA tracks the Dow Jones index we all hear about on the news and in the papers. It is only thirty stocks and is therefore considered "concentrated." What is nice about the fund is the current yield and low annual fees. The annual yield is 4.38 percent _after_ the annual management fee of 0.17 percent. This yield is almost identical to the yield on a 30-year Treasury bond. So if we did enter a bear market you can collect as much income as the risk-free return of a T-bond and get growth potential.

> **ETF: Exchange-Traded Fund:**
> "A security that tracks an index, a commodity or a basket of assets…but trades like a stock."
>
> Source: Investopedia.com

IWV is much more diverse, tracking about 86 percent of the U.S. stock market. So you will get all sizes of stocks, all major styles of investing and all industries. It contains over 2,900 different stocks. The annual fee is low at 0.21 percent but also yields less than the first fund at 1.47 percent annually.

Both of these funds should be considered only a slice of your portfolio. They are not investing cure-alls. They are just the beginning of a smart allocation.

Originally published in July, 2010.

How to Pick a Mutual Fund

A STRONG FOUNDATION

As you might know I strongly believe in the many, many benefits of mutual funds. While you can have more tax control, hands-on selection and excitement with individual stocks you give up other benefits. With a fund you get professional management, extreme diversification and lower general volatility. You also get convenience, low minimum investments, trading-cost economies and better research available to institutional investors. You can also sleep better at night not worrying if you are in the next Enron.

Before you pick your own funds you should have a strong foundation in the form of a personalized asset allocation.

Yes, asset allocation does work. For example, if

you invested $10,000 into **BlackRock Asset Allocation** fund (symbol: PCLAX) over the last decade you would have $15,633. The same investment over this "lost decade" in the S&P 500 index would be $9,090.

FREE TOOLS

It is hard to consistently pick winning stocks but simple to pick funds. There are a lot of free sites that are helpful. The granddaddy of them all is **Morningstar.com**. That is where I got the allocation fund performance. Another useful site is **CEFConnect.com**. This site specializes in closed-end fund research. Another site is **Zacks.com**. Zacks is stock-centered but they have nice "Top 5" lists. Their lists high-light some pretty interesting funds and can be a good place to start your research.

GOOD, FREE SITES

- Morningstar.com
- CEFConnect.com
- Zacks.com
- WSJ.com

WHAT TO LOOK FOR

What most people look at first is yearly expenses. Expenses are very important so you should look closely. Compare them to other similar funds to get an apples-to-apples comparison.

When I look at Morningstar I pay even closer attention to their style boxes. Here you can see what the managers are actually investing in. Are they **called** a small-company fund but really invest in mid-sized companies? The style box will tell. This will help you build true diversification.

Looking at the top holdings of the fund can also help you to see what the management is really investing in.

Also look at the portfolio turnover. This is how often the manager is trading. The higher the turnover percent the more trading. The more trading the more expenses to you.

LOOKING AT INCOME

A key component of investing is producing income. With your funds you should look at the current yields. Also look at the past income. This will give you a picture of historic payouts for the fund. Is the income trending up? Or down?

Look at the details and arm yourself with information.

Originally published in August, 2010.

Don't Dread Deflation

The latest economic gossip floating around the media is the much-hyped, much-feared deflation. We've all heard of it. We've all heard it's not good. Is that really true?

Like most things financial there isn't a simple yes or no answer. If you have long-term deflation (prices going down) it's very bad. It's like Japan…two decades of stagnation. That lack of growth has made it easier for China to surpass Japan as the second largest economy recently.

> **Deflation**—"A general decline in prices, often caused by a reduction in the supply of money or credit. Deflation can be caused also by a decrease in government, personal or investment spending."
>
> Investopedia.com

On the other hand, if a nation has had too much inflation then there might be a need for prices to go down for a while. Popping this inflationary bubble is an important task of our recent recession.

INFLATION TAKES A BREAK

Think about the last ten years. Wasn't it almost expected that things would cost more every other time we went to the store? Or bought some clothes? Or filled up our gas tanks? Or looked for a new car? Or, especially, looked for a new house?

These are very general examples. But wasn't that what it felt like?

We're hearing a lot about deflation because three months in a row inflation was down. But if you add up those three months it's barely 0.4 percent lower. Pretty small. Also, for the full twelve months ended this July inflation was actually up 1.2 percent (source: BLS.gov). By definition that's the opposite of deflation.

STEPS TO TAKE

If you run across any articles on this you may read some of their suggestions for investing. Usually they're pretty general or say to invest in U.S. government bonds. That's part of the solution.

It's actually very simple to profit from this scenario.

Because things go down in value our purchasing power is finally going up. So simply invest for high income. If you have a fixed investment income of 7 percent then you are able to buy more with that 7 percent when (and if) things drop in value.

It also comes down to having a diverse mix of income assets to create that cash flow. That way you are prepared for the many other scenarios that can happen in the investing world.

After all, who really knows what's going to happen next? Just be prepared for everything.

Originally published in September, 2010.

MAKING THE GRADE

It is that time of year again. Kids and grandkids are back to school. There are even a lot of adults going back to school to enhance those job skills. With school comes the infamous report card.

IF COUNTRIES HAD REPORT CARDS

I was wondering how the U.S. stacks up against the rest of the world financially. Because we're a mature economy I decided to measure "the States" against five other developed countries and grade them. I did not include emerging economies like China and Brazil. They are smaller economies, growing faster and in a realm of their own. The five countries we will compare to the U.S. are Japan, Germany, France, the United Kingdom and Canada.

All five economies are similarly diverse, grow at similar levels and have similar political structures. They even have comparable ages of population due to a Baby Boom.

We will measure three subjects: markets, economy and financial responsibility.

SUBJECT ONE: MARKETS

Just like the U.S., our five friends have a major stock market index. For the U.S. we have the S&P 500, the Nikkei 225 in Japan and the CAC 40 in France. We will use the price-to-earnings ratio and the year-to-date return of the respective countries to make the final grade (Source: Bloomberg.com).

The P/E ratio is a common way to figure value. Most every one agrees that the lower this ratio the better the value. If there is a low P/E ratio then that investment is earning more money and is selling at a lower price.

The P/Es ranged from a low of 13 (France) to a high of almost 24 (Japan). The stock market returns went from negative nine (Japan) to plus 9.6 percent (Germany). The U.S. had a 14.7 P/E and a return of over 5 percent this year.

SUBJECT TWO: ECONOMY

For this subject, we will use 2009 GDP (Gross Domestic Product), 2015 estimated GDP and the percent growth between the two years. Data is from the *International Monetary Fund* (IMF).

The U.S. was at the very top of the class. We had the highest GDP for 2009 ($14.8 trillion), the highest GDP for 2015 estimates ($18.2 trillion) and near the top in percentage growth with a 23 percent increase. The bottom grade was held by France only because of slow growth estimated for the next six years. The UK and Canada had the highest percent growth (both at 27 percent).

SUBJECT THREE: FINANCIAL RESPONSIBILITY

For our final subject we have two key stats: government debt as a percent of GDP (high is bad) and savings rates. Both are for 2009, with data from the OECD (*Organization for Economic Cooperation and Development*) and the IMF.

Again at the bottom of the class is Japan. They have the highest debt ratio, at 189 percent of their GDP. The U.S. was top of the class with the lowest debt-to-GDP (53 percent).

THE FINAL GRADES:				
	Markets	Economy	F.R.	Overall:
Japan:	D	B+	D	C-
Germany:	A	B	B	B+
France:	B	C	B+	B
UK:	B	B	C-	B-
Canada:	C+	B	C-	B-
USA:	B	A+	C+	B+

STILL HEAD OF THE CLASS

Despite all of the recent financial turmoil, the U.S. is still competitive with our peers. We may not grow as quickly as the emerging underclassmen, but we have a sizable economy that continues to expand and our markets look like a good value.

Here's to graduation day!

Originally published in October, 2010.

How to Pick a Financial Advisor

This weekend I read an article in *The Wall Street Journal*. It went over the hundreds and hundreds of designations financial reps use. There can be a virtual alphabet soup after a professionals' name.

The article had some important points like which credentials are best (CFA, CPA and CFP) and which are "least rigorous" (CRFA, CSA and CSFP).

One thing it did not mention was the importance of getting advice. Most investors would serve themselves well if they get some kind of advice. The results are there. According to Forrester Research, "four in five U.S. millionaires use a financial advisor." Also, study after study shows that investors with no help at all underperformed the market significantly. But who can we trust?

WHO MOST OF US WILL RUN INTO

As far as professionals managing money, most

people will be exposed to three main types: insurance agents, stockbrokers and financial advisors. They might have one or a dozen credentials after their name but most fall into these three categories.

INSURANCE AGENTS

Two of my good neighbors are insurance agents and are like most agents. They are hard-working, ethical and honest. They hold a state license to sell insurance products like term-life, long-term care and health insurance.

Despite having a license investors should still be diligent in researching an agent and understanding their limitations. I see many national ads from agents claiming they are "advisors". This is very misleading. The only thing they can give advice on is insurance. They also do not have a fiduciary duty. This means they do <u>not</u> need to put the interests of the investor or consumer first.

STOCKBROKERS

Any time you see one of the big-name brokerage companies most of their reps will be stockbrokers. They have passed a test called the Series 7. This test covers most "paper" assets like stocks, bonds and mutual funds. It even goes into alternative assets like gold and commodities and topics like taxes and investment strategies.

> **"A fiduciary is required to act in the best interests of the person he or she is working with."**
>
> Investopedia.com

Are they fiduciaries? There is a trend in the industry to start holding these licenses to a fiduciary standard but currently they do <u>not</u> need to put the investor first in their recommendations. Technically, they have a duty <u>first</u> to their brokerage company.

FINANCIAL ADVISORS

These professionals can call themselves financial advisors. They are licensed as such and they <u>are</u> fiduciaries. The Investment Adviser's Act of 1940 defines this role of loyalty to the client very explicitly. They must put the client's interests ahead of their own.

A financial advisor must first pass the Series 7 and then can take the Series 66 test. This covers economics, investment vehicles and strategies, ethics and state laws.

Of the three credentials favored by *The Wall Street Journal*, only one is now held to a fiduciary standard (since 2008). All three professionals are highly trained and are more challenging to become than most of the other credentials. Investors would be in very competent hands going with any of these three or a financial advisor.

Originally published in November, 2010.

GM Makes a Comeback

"LIKE A PHOENIX OUT OF THE ASHES"

As I write this, GM has just sold new stock to the public. They raised at least $20 billion and it could be as high as $23.1 billion (source: Bloomberg.com). If they raise the higher amount it will place the U.S. back at the top of biggest IPOs (initial public offerings), passing China's recent record. I hope they do it.

It was a good thing that GM could declare bankruptcy. It saved thousands of jobs, it maintained precious confidence in a very bad economy <u>and</u> the U.S. government can actually <u>make billions</u> off of the deal.

Besides that, it also highlights the efficiencies of the U.S. system. An institution like GM can prosper for decades, enrich its' native country and reinvent itself after stumbling down. That kind of tolerance for failure makes the U.S. continually innovative and flexible as an economy.

IS THIS ALL POSITIVE?

For recent stock and bond investors the GM bankruptcy was anything but good. As far as my research shows, the stock investors received a 100% loss. Some bond investors made out a little better. One of the last bond prices was 32.5 cents for every dollar invested (a 67.5% loss).

Fortunately, we can learn some basics from this event.

LESSONS FOR INVESTORS

Lesson #1: Do Your Research

Of course, always invest the time to thoroughly look at a companies' balance sheet, industry trends, cash levels, etc. The most important stat is the potential investments' debt level. If you see a very steady and dramatic rise is long-term debt you need to think twice and then three times before investing.

Lesson #2: (The Old Standby) Diversify

You've heard it a thousand times before. You probably get tired of hearing that same advice repeated over and over. Diversify. Warren Buffetts' mentor Ben Graham was a big believer in this. Warren himself oversees more than 70 companies and dozens of additional investments. Diversify.

Lesson #3: Use Mutual Funds

What is the easiest way to efficiently diversify? Use a mutual fund. Individual stocks and bonds can be more tax-efficient and you do have more control of buying and selling. Yet a fund can offer extreme diversification at very low internal costs. Funds have additional disclosures that are required by law; making them very transparent investments (always remember the lack of transparency with Madoff). They can mimic an index, offering a passive investment in hundreds of individual securities. Or they offer professional management, constantly adjusting the portfolio. Pretty good benefits.

Think again of the Old GM investors. Would you rather lose 67% of your single bond investment or be in a mutual fund that owns 400 <u>different</u> bonds? If one bond defaults out of the group then your loss is 0.25 percent. It seems pretty clear which would help an investor sleep better at night.

Originally published in December, 2010.

FINALLY BULLISH

After ten years of bubbles and catastrophes this advisor is starting to get a little bullish.

We have experienced a lot of calamity over the last ten years. We have had bubbles, ranging from the Dot.com run-up, to the housing bubble and credit crisis, and currently the commodities bubble. Of course, we have also had disasters like 9/11 and The Great Recession.

What has been the impact on the market? Towards the start of the last decade the S&P 500 experienced three negative years in a row (2000-2002). That only occurs roughly every four decades. Big news on its own. Then the whole decade was negative. That was HUGE news. A negative decade for the S&P 500 is a "two-century" event. Very rare.

These last ten years would make just about anyone down on the market and the economy. With all of these bubbles swirling around I have never been bullish, either.

THERE IS A SILVER LINING...

One big money manager, billionaire Bill Gross, firmly believes in a "new normal." By new normal he means low GDP growth and high unemployment forever. I think that is nonsense. America has a dynamic, multi-layered economy that prizes innovation and growth. That is our saving grace.

I heard recently we can even balance the Federal budget by 2014 by simply freezing government spending. How could that be? Because America is a...dynamic, multi-layered and growing economy.

There is a technical term that sums up my new optimism. It is called "reverting to the mean." That is a fancy way for saying returning to normal. After such extreme events this "rule" says we should expect a more normalized market return. We <u>could</u> even experience better-than-average returns in the next several years. Although I would be happy with normal yearly returns in the eight to ten percent range.

SUPPORT FROM THE IMF

This is not just blind confidence, either. The *International Monetary Fund* has estimates for our GDP. From 2011 to 2015 we are estimated to hit new, never-before-seen highs in our economy. Going from an estimated $14.6 trillion in 2010 to $18 trillion by 2015.

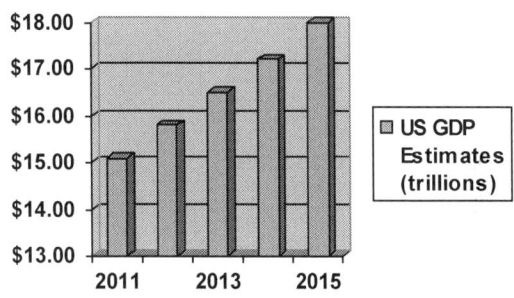

IN GOOD COMPANY

There are always opposing views about the future. There are some very passionate pessimists like Bill Gross. But there are some other optimists. Another billionaire money manager, Ken Fisher, went so far as to call Gross' new normal "idiotic." Fisher also alluded to more growth ahead, saying, "Get ready for this market's second leg."

More level-headed optimism has come from Warren Buffett, saying recently "I am a huge bull on this country." Even Fed Chairman Ben Bernanke has said "…it is reasonable to expect some pickup in growth in 2011 and in subsequent years."

HOW TO PROFIT

What does all of this mean? It could mean risk will once more pay better than safety. If you have been using the mattress for your investments now could be a good time to slowly increase your exposure to the market.

Of course, always have a smart allocation plan and diversify with unique asset classes.

Happy New Year!

Originally published in January, 2011.

5 Investor Moves for the New Year

Take these steps to clean up your portfolio, lower your investment risk and position your nest egg for new gains.

There is no better time than the New Year to groom your portfolio. We have already had a few good years in the stock market and some great years in the metal and bond markets. Now may be the time to consider some of these steps.

1. RE-BALANCE YOUR GAINS

I hope 2010 left you with some good gains on your investments. A key to locking in those profits is re-balancing. For example, if you have $10,000 in a mutual fund and it is now $12,000 then sell the two-thousand dollar increase.

This way you still have the bigger part of the position, you have limited your exposure to an appreciated (and possibly overpriced) asset class <u>and</u> you have "locked in" your gain. If the fund drops you have your $2,000 profit out.

2. SLOWLY INCREASE EXPOSURE TO "RISK" ASSETS

I believe the stock market will finally respond with some respectable and lasting growth. The previous two years have been up and this year could continue positively. We will definitely see volatility throughout this time. But…we could see increased risk-taking rewarded.

The main "risk" assets are stocks in all of their flavors. Some examples are small-company, mid-sized, sector, real estate and international equities. Improving markets usually benefit these riskier classes.

I would avoid the areas that have gone up too much. For example, gold and other precious metals, certain international markets or high-priced (low-earning) individual stocks.

FIVE NEW YEAR MOVES:

1. **RE-BALANCE**
2. **MORE STOCKS**
3. **LESS GOV'T BONDS**
4. **LOWER MATURITIES**
5. **LEARN MORE**

---

3. ALLOCATE LESS TO GOVERNMENT BONDS

Federal interest rates are at their lowest in history. Up is really the only way for them to move...eventually.

What bond sector usually gets hit the hardest when rates change? Often U.S. Treasury bonds get whipsawed during interest rate moves. So keep a smaller amount in this area.

4. LOWER BOND & CD MATURITIES

For the same reason you want less government bonds you want to lower the overall maturity of other fixed income investments. Fixed income values can be unstable during rate moves.

Also, the last thing you would want to do now is lock in a long-term CD. It might be tempting compared to other low-yielding investments. But when rates jump up that 10- or 20-year CD will pale in comparison. Keep these maturities short.

5. LEARN MORE

Always inform yourself. There are vast free resources on the internet that will help you make decisions or help you start a conversation with your advisor.

Some of the better sites are <u>Morningstar.com</u> and <u>Investopedia.com</u>. The first site has good articles, in-depth tools for understanding your portfolio and helpful investment-specific details. Investopedia is my favorite. It has articles covering basic to advanced topics, tutorials, a stock simulation game and acts as an encyclopedia of investing.

*   *   *

    Any of these steps can help you improve your portfolio. Do not stop with these ideas. As you know, the investing landscape is <u>always</u> moving. Pay special attention to idea number five and continually update your investment IQ.

Originally published in February, 2011.

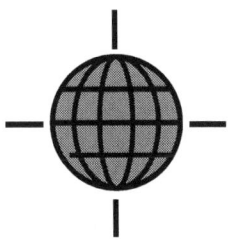

Australia: Gateway to Asia Riches?

This island continent has a developed economy that can literally fuel the continual growth in emerging Asian countries.

Is there a way to "play" the emerging economies of Asia with possibly less risk than a direct investment? There may be.

Australia is a developed country that has a very lucky geography. They are in the new sweet spot of the emerging world economy.

This area of the world has significantly higher growth than older economies like Europe, Japan and the U.S. And it looks like that growth will continue.

Why is Australia so Well Positioned?

Politically, economically and demographically they are a developed country. They have the 13th largest economy in the world at $1.3 trillion, a low unemployment rate, low inflation and a sizeable population. In other words, they may be less risky than investing into only China or other individual markets.

They are also a big exporter of basic goods, ranging from agriculture to mining. In fact, 57% of their exports come from these two industries. They are a commodity-based exporter. Those goods are in high demand from China, India and others. They need to have these goods to keep growing.

How Do You Invest Into Australia?

A great thing about our financial markets is innovation. A lot of innovation comes from the mutual fund industry. There are new funds created every month based on different strategies or tactics. One type of exchange-traded fund (ETF) is the country-specific fund.

The Australian ETF is called **iShares MSCI Australia Index** fund (symbol: **EWA**). The fund is traded on the stock exchange so an investor can buy and sell it any time during trading hours, borrow against it on margin and even short the shares if you believe it will go down. These last two features are very aggressive and I do not personally recommend them. But investors do have that flexibility.

Some Stats on the Fund From Morningstar.com

This fund has a nice dividend, paying 3.35% yearly. That is almost as much income as an investor would get from a 30-year Treasury bond with growth potential as a bonus. It has a very low internal expense of 0.53% per year. It has a mix of 73 different stock holdings, blending both growth and value companies.

There Are Risks...

Some of the good points about Australia are their bad points, too. Because they export so much in commodities they are negatively affected when commodity prices drop.

Their exports to four countries account for 56% of total exports. This makes Australia very reliant on the health of those economies. If these trade partners dip Australia is probably not far behind.

Investing in a single country mutual fund also has risks. It is concentrated and should be considered a small part of an overall asset allocation, including many unique asset classes.

* * *

Australia has many advantages and may be poised to piggy-back Asia's growth. But be careful, look at other ways to play emerging markets and let this be the start of your research Down Under.

Originally published in March, 2011.

Two Ways to Pick a Stock

There are many factors to look at and consider when investigating an individual stock. You can look at volume, price, earnings-per-share, different ratios, debt and a lot more. Here are two that are very important.

1. Think About the Business Model

A business model is the basic method of conducting business for a company. An example is Dell Computers. What is their business model? They sell computers direct to consumers and businesses, bypassing the retail channel. What is Office Max's business model? They sell office supplies, including computers, to consumers and businesses using retail stores and some website sales.

One product (computers) and two models. This model difference affects their balance sheet, net income, revenue and almost every other financial aspect.

You can learn a lot about a companies' potential for success and survival by understanding their business model. What company probably has a greater chance of survival in an economic downturn (all other things being equal)? A company that sells a low-priced service that a great number of consumers need monthly or a company that sells a high-priced product that only needs to be replaced every five or more years? I would put my money on the low-priced, monthly-replaced business model.

2. Consider Companies with High Earnings Yields

The earnings yield is the opposite of the P/E ratio. It is essentially the E/P ratio. You divide a companies' total earnings by the total market price of the stock.

For example, if ABC Widget Company has annual earnings of $20 million and a market value of $200 million, then the earnings yield would be 0.10 (or 10%). So for every dollar of market value the company is earning ten cents.

How do you spot potential value with the earnings yield?

Imagine a popular company that everyone adores is making $1 billion dollars every year in net income. That looks very good. But if that business was valued on the stock market for $100 billion the earnings yield would be a paltry one percent! For every dollar invested, the company is actually only producing one penny in net income for you, the shareholder and part-owner.

It could be a great company that is well-managed

and liked by the public and probably growing. But is it a smart investment?

Let's look at the other side. Imagine a different company earning the same $1 billion annually and valued on the stock market at only $5 billion dollars. That would give you an earnings yield of 20 percent. Can you see the better value? For every dollar invested in this stock, the shareholder receives the benefit from twenty cents in earnings.

Since we compare net earnings to market price, we get a more-accurate measure of value <u>to the shareholder</u>. Because of this, I consider the earnings yield the **True Shareholder Net Profit** © and the BEST measure of stock value.

Good luck spotting those worthy stocks.

Originally published in April, 2011.

ONE-TIME RODNEY DANGERFIELD OF INVESTMENTS NOW INDUSTRY BEHEMOTH

A milestone has been reached. According to *The Wall Street Journal*, a relatively new type of investment has grown fairly big. This investment now has about $1.4 <u>trillion</u> dollars in assets. That is quite a few zeros. What is it? An ETF.

ETF stands for exchange-traded fund. These funds are just one of the several branches to the mutual fund family tree. Funds have a lot going for them.

Here is a re-cap of mutual fund benefits:

- Professional management
- Instant diversity

- Reasonable fees
- Passive investing

Keep in mind there are more types of mutual funds than this new arrival. Below are the main mutual fund types. Each has good points and drawbacks. A combination of them all in a portfolio can make sense.

Let Them Eat Vanilla

When most of us talk about funds we are referring to the plain-vanilla, open-ended mutual fund. This type has a long history stretching back to the 1920s. They have trillions and trillions in assets. The big player on the block.

Some open-end mutual fund benefits:

- Relatively low trading volatility
- No or low sales charges
- Most-varied investment strategies

Because of their once-daily trading, open-end fund investors can be late to liquidate or buy. While the rest of the stock and bond market has been humming all day, these investors are stuck to the last trades of the day. They can also have high internal expenses.

Where the Innovation Happens

Exchange-traded funds have grown in popularity for good reason. Most of the current innovation is occurring in the ETF arena. New approaches are literally entering the market every month. Some of these strategies can be very aggressive so do your research.

Here are some pluses:

- Trades all day like a stock—easy to buy and sell
- Can margin (borrow) against
- Relatively low internal management expenses

Sale on Aisle Three

One of my personal favorites is the little-followed, rarely-used closed-end mutual fund. They can be thinly traded. With very little trading activity investors can get stuck with accepting whatever price is available when selling. They, like open-end funds, can have fairly high internal expenses.

Closed-end funds are the only category where you can buy the proverbial dollar for ninety cents. For example, ABC Closed Fund might sell in the open market for $9 per share while having assets of $10 per share.

Caveat Emptor

As you can see, even something that might seem simple can have multiple layers. So take the time to do the research.

Some good places to start are Morningstar.com and CEFConnect.com. The first site will cover all fund types but is stronger in open-end and ETF research. CEFConnect.com specializes in closed-end funds.

Keep your eyes open for the next big thing. It could be just a trend or a force to be reckoned with like exchange-traded funds.

Originally published in May, 2011.

How to Lower Your Gold Risk

Big volatility is happening in commodities markets, most of it in speculative precious metals. Silver has dropped about 30 percent, cocoa dropped roughly 17 percent and even gold had a mild tumble. Although I agree with the **reasons** why commodities have moved up, the higher they go the higher the risk gets.

Good Idea to Have Inflation Protection

Gold has done great for over a decade. Why? Because of the **expectation** of inflation. Inflation is really a weakening dollar. And investors should protect, or hedge, against this.

Is there a smarter, lower-risk way to protect against these risks?

Use a Mutual Fund

If I had to choose between owning **one** gold mining stock or a mutual fund with **203** gold mining stocks, I would choose and recommend the fund.

Why use a mutual fund, which may be less tax-efficient and fee-efficient instead of individual stocks? Just remember what happened to Enron. Or the Old GM. Or fill in the blank with a dotcom stock from 1999 that does not exist today.

While a fund does not guarantee profits, it usually spreads risk **and** gives enough exposure to a particular asset.

"Go Wide!"

In place of gold stocks, bullion or a gold fund, consider a broad-based commodities fund. There are more and more entering the market regularly, giving wider choices. These funds usually provide gold exposure, too.

According to Registered Rep magazine, the Dow Jones-AIG Commodity Index tracks 19 different materials. Energy, precious and industrial metals, agriculturals and livestock are part of the index. The iPath Dow Jones-Commodity Fund (symbol: DJP) tracks this index and is easy to purchase.

My favorite, the Rogers International Commodity Index, tracks 38 commodities, making it the most diverse index in the category. It was created by a legendary investor: Jim Rogers. He co-managed hedge funds with billionaire George Soros and travelled the globe on his motorcycle in search of investments. His index is tracked as an ELEMENTS fund (symbol: RJI).

Limit Your Exposure

It is a good idea to guard against a weak dollar, possible high inflation and a slow economy. But as a sector, like commodities, goes up, it is equally important to sell gains. Selling limits the percentage of your portfolio exposed to this "hot" area.

Most importantly, you want a **reasonable** amount invested to begin with. It would be over-exposure to have half of your portfolio in a commodity fund. Any amount over 10 percent can be too much. Remember that commodities are **more** volatile than stocks.

A Different Environment

Inflation fears, low interest rates and economic meltdowns have created an ideal environment for this current materials run-up. What happens when inflation fears ease, interest rates rise and economies boom again? A different environment moves in and creates volatility in "sure things" of the past.

Guard against future risks with these three ideas. Happy investing.

Originally published in June, 2011.

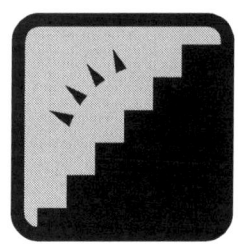

THE 3-STEP NO-BRAINER MUTUAL FUND STRATEGY

This concept is so deceptively simple and easy to start you might not take it seriously. It could save you hundreds or thousands of dollars in fees and commissions. Wall Street would prefer you to NOT read this article for fear of losing business.

This approach is straightforward, can be used as a stand-alone strategy and is easy to manage. If this is your only investment it can pay off handsomely for you if allowed to work as described.

STEP ONE: Invest in a Balanced Mutual Fund or Asset Allocation Fund

A balanced fund is a combination of assets. It is usually a blend of stocks, bonds and cash. You might see the word "balanced" in the name of the fund. For example, it could be called "Dreydelity Balanced Fund".

It could even include international stocks and bonds, real estate or other types of investments and therefore could be an asset allocation fund. Both types will work.

The key is to have the diversification of various asset classes. This will provide a one-stop investment for the long haul that can be held for years with minimal maintenance.

STEP TWO: Dollar-Cost Average Into the Fund & Invest More as it Drops in Value

Invest a fixed amount monthly, dollar-cost average, to buy more shares when the market is down and less over-priced shares when the market is too pricey.

When the price drops significantly, as in a "bear" market, you add <u>even more</u> than the usual amount. By doing that, you are making market volatility work *for you*. And accumulating cheap shares for future growth.

STEP THREE: Invest for Fifteen or More Years

Why fifteen years? According to *Ibbotson Associates, Inc.*, from the years 1926-2000, you would have had a 100% chance of profit if you had invested in stocks and held for fifteen or more years. Yes, you read that correctly; you would have been *assured* a positive return.

But what about the awful stock market returns in the last decade? According to website *MoneyChimp.com*, even the last 15 years would have produced a 6.72% average annual return.

You can now see how flawed it is when someone equates the stock market with gambling. I would much rather have those odds than a Vegas slot machine.

These years also include many <u>huge</u> events like The Great Depression, Pearl Harbor bombing, JFK assassination, frequent recessions, high interest rates, the Dot-Com Bubble, The Great Recession, a "lost decade" in stocks and much more.

In addition, with this strategy we are using bonds and cash which produce regular income **and** lower volatility, helping to balance our returns in each period.

* * *

"Everything should be made as simple as possible, but not simpler."

—Albert Einstein

Originally published in July, 2011.

How to Avoid Bad Information

Today is a great time to have a question. You can find a million answers at your fingertips either through the internet and mobile phones or traditional channels like magazines, papers and newsletters.

With so many potential sources remember to follow the old proverb of taking advice "with a grain of salt." Here are a few ways to get those trusty, high-quality answers you might be seeking.

1. Listen to Qualified Media

There are some big brands peddling information to the public such as CNBC, Bloomberg, Wall Street Journal, Financial Times and Fox Business. All of these brands have some great content to offer but also tend to have a political leaning. Sometimes these leanings can lead to extreme opinions that stray from the facts or focus on the "convenient" facts needed for their viewpoint.

Solution? Use many of these sources to create a balanced view.

2. Listen to Qualified Experts

The internet is a great spreader of information. We can access info on every subject imaginable. If I don't understand something about apricot trees I just look up Wikipedia.com and—BAM!—instant expert! It reminds me of the Holiday Inn commercials a few years back where an accountant can perform surgery because he is now so smart after his hotel stay.

It is a bit scary: the internet has made every website operator, Blogger, Twitterer and Facebooker a potential expert. Are they? Of course not. It's more important now than ever to look for licensed experts or experts with a lot of experience. Or both.

3. Avoid Most Paid Newsletters

I like newsletters. They can be a good source of information and are usually written by a truly qualified expert. Yet they tend to focus only on one investment type such as dividend-paying stocks or commodities, for example.

Focusing on only one or two assets can lead to overinvestment in those areas and an unbalanced portfolio, overweight in potentially risky assets. It can also create too much activity that racks up fees and builds a bad investment position.

Taking these newsletters too seriously can produce

big losses. If these experts were so certain of their "picks" then why are they selling a newsletter? They could be on the beach with all of their personal investing profits....

Solution? Read any newsletters available to you and gather good ideas to start researching. Consider them <u>potential</u> investments that require solid research <u>before</u> committing money.

4. Stick with a Long-Term Plan

If you have a healthy, balanced portfolio that represents many different asset classes and is, hopefully, producing a nice income then you should be able to avoid these sensational opinions in the media.

It is always good to keep an open mind to investment information and to try to avoid major market catastrophes. But there will always be those "black swan" events that no one expert consistently predicts.

* * *

"True genius resides in the capacity for evaluation of uncertain, hazardous, and conflicting information."

—Winston Churchill

Originally published in August, 2011.

"WE THE DEBTORS...

...Of the United States of America."

We have all heard about the disastrous debt downgrade of our nation. But is it justified? This is a very heated topic that quickly becomes political. My vague answer is "yes" and "no." The downgrade makes sense but I feel it is not entirely accurate.

Standard & Poor's has quite a bit of justification for lowering the rating. We have our highest national debt levels in history. We have the biggest future obligations in history. We have low tax revenue. We have weak and impotent political spirit. And on and on.

But is S&P the best judge of credit? I do not know the specific, complex process that credit agencies use but S&P does not have the best batting average. They recently rated toxic mortgages as AAA, the very highest credit quality. We know how that turned out.

They also downgraded Berkshire Hathaway, Warren Buffett's holding company, from the pristine AAA, to the next lowest AA+ rating. Why did they downgrade Buffett? Mainly because he bought BNSF Railroad. About a year later the company's cash on hand is back up to **over** $40 billion **and** they own a profitable railroad. Berkshire looks stronger than ever, not suffering a credit crisis.

As a side note, Buffett very publicly said the U.S. deserves a quadruple-A credit rating. Maybe he is still sour over his downgrade....

* * *

The bottom line still remains. The U.S. is saddled with an unmanageable amount of current and future debt. And the trend is obviously moving upward. That is essentially why we were downgraded.

This vote of no confidence created an absurd result. The very debt that was knocked down was bought hand over fist. Treasury bonds recently sold for a 14 percent premium. For every $1,000 of bonds investors were shelling out $1,140 in cash to purchase them. At maturity, in 30 years, those bonds will only pay the $1,000 face value. A guaranteed loss of principal?!

Why would anyone invest in that?

I think The Sage of Omaha was onto something. When there is panic in the markets, whether international or local, people usually flock to Treasury debt. U.S. bonds are the only investment that I, as a stockbroker and financial advisor, can <u>still</u> legally call risk free. That is because of the strength of our economy, our taxing power and because we have never defaulted on debt or interest. Maybe we should be AAAA-rated.

* * *

"Contracting debt will almost infallibly be abused in every government."

—David Hume

"A national debt, if it is not excessive, will be to us a national blessing."

—Alexander Hamilton

Originally published in September, 2011.

THE #1 INVESTING TECHNIQUE

What is the most important investing technique available? Is it technical or fundamental analysis? Is it value or growth investing? Is it low P/E investing? Or momentum investing? Or alternative assets like commodities? The answer: **psychology.**

Three investing-psychology biggies are accurate thinking, informed decision-making and calculated risk-taking. These skills will help you filter through the media clutter, bad advice, lies and emotions that come along with the game of investing.

Principle 1: Accurate Thinking

While speaking with investors, I run across many deeply-held misconceptions. Some think that CDs are the safest investment. They are not. They are subject to interest-rate risk and inflation risk. Some believe in guaranteed real estate investments. As we have seen recently, real estate is anything but stable and definitely not guaranteed. Some think they are diverse if they own 8 different mutual funds. They may not be if those funds are holding similar or identical investments.

To have accurate thinking, you need investing knowledge. Not everyone has this solid foundation. If you need more fundamentals, you can contact me and request a free copy of my first book, *Investing To Win*. I wrote this 100-page book as if I was giving investing basics to my kids. I wanted it factual and easy-to-read. This will give you the groundwork needed for accurate thinking.

Principle 2: Informed Decision-Making

The most vital part to this principle is information. Make sure you are getting high-quality information from a variety of respected sources. Then do your own thinking.

Another crucial piece is emotions. For example, an investor has two different advisors. One is more likeable than the other. He has better "bedside manner" and is more polished. Yet, the second advisor provides more and better information and does not exaggerate claims. This is a moment to gain control of our emotions and work with the more-informative advisor.

More emotional roadblocks are market swings and advances. If the market has already dropped significantly, it is probably too late to sell. The damage is done. Should an investor still sell low, on emotion, only to buy back later at a higher price?!

Be informed and in control. Why was Warren Buffett buying during The Great Recession and this recent market correction? He is in control of his investor psychology.

Principle 3: Calculated Risk-Taking

Another risk is opportunity cost. That means if an investor plays it too safe they may be missing growth opportunities.

The S&P 500 companies are expected to be at historic high earnings this year and next year. The U.S. economy is estimated to be higher every year up to, and including, the year 2016.

Now could be the time to ignore the pessimism, pull the money from the mattress and consider more calculated risks.

*　*　*

"We simply attempt to be fearful when others are greedy and to be greedy only when others are fearful."

—Warren Buffett

"A woman's guess is much more accurate than a man's certainty."

—Rudyard Kipling

Originally published in October, 2011.

Ten Biggest Investor Mistakes: Part 1

There are many common mistakes we all can make from time to time. Try to avoid these first five and remember to stay tuned for part two of this article.

1. Investing in Variable Annuities When Not Suitable

After reviewing hundreds of investors' portfolios this is the very biggest error I have noticed. Please don't take this the wrong way. For the right person in the right situation with the right goals a low-cost annuity can be appropriate. For most people, I think it is unnecessary. The annual fees can have a bad effect on investment performance, sometimes costing over four percent a year of your total assets!

2. Not Having Personal Disability Insurance

According to a recent article in *Money* magazine, you are more than twice as likely to become disabled before age 65 than to die prematurely. The article continued on with some very good advice when looking for a disability policy: make sure the coverage lasts until age 65 or older; that it covers inability to do your specific job and not complete disability from any job; and, to lower the cost, have a two to three month waiting time before you would receive your benefits.

3. Acting on "Hot" Investment Tips

We have all probably received well-meaning tips and advice from friends and family. You can sometimes get good insights from these sources, keeping an open mind to new ideas. But it can be dangerous to your financial health to act on these tips without getting qualified advice and conducting your own research and due diligence.

4. Not Preparing a Comprehensive Estate and Financial Plan

Your life is busy and growing more complex everyday. There is more information packed into the Sunday edition of *The New York Times* newspaper than a person received in their entire life during the fifteenth-century. Your financial life is a reflection of that. You may have many aspects that should be taken care of: children, grandchildren, *great* grandchildren, business equity, cash flow management, retirement, college for your offspring and many other considerations. What you can do is have a complete financial plan drafted up by a qualified financial advisor. You can consult an attorney for a will or trust and other legal documents. Remember to include insurance planning and reviews for total protection.

5. Not Asking Enough of the Right Questions

When it comes to your money and future there is no unintelligent question. You should be fully informed by your advisor. Some questions to ask regarding investments: *"What are the total annual fees? Are there charges to enter and exit the investment? How much?"*

A few questions to ask about your consultant: *"How are you compensated? What is your investment philosophy? What do you invest in? Are you a fiduciary?"* You may want to write out these questions and others that are important to you.

* * *

"Questions are never indiscreet, answers sometimes are."

—Oscar Wilde

Originally published in November, 2011.

Ten Biggest Investor Mistakes: Part 2

Thank you very much for returning for part two of this article. Here is the next set of common investor mistakes to avoid.

6. Setting Aside Too Little for Retirement

Depending on your age, desired retirement income, risk tolerance and many other factors, you should have a clear idea of the number of dollars you need to set aside to reach your goals. Talk with a trustworthy advisor to come up with an adequate amount that accounts for different scenarios, like flat or down markets. When you reach your goals, you should make sure you are invested in the right asset mix to **maintain** your income.

7. Investing Only in One Asset Class or Country

We all have our favorite investments. For some, it might be real estate or small stocks or international bonds, although we should not be limited to **only one** investment. This happened disastrously in the late 1990s when most people were mainly in large growth companies. Then what happened? For three years straight, most suffered declines. Many people lost half or more of their principal! Further back, in the 1980s, a lot of investors were over-weighted in real estate. What resulted? Interest rates went "to the sky", many real estate fortunes were lost and many bankruptcies were declared. It is vitally important to fully diversify into multiple asset classes.

8. Paying Too Much in Taxes on Their Portfolios

You are efficient in your life and you need to be with your investments, as well. There are many efficient ways to minimize your investment tax bill.

Using tax-deferred and tax-exempt investments whenever possible is one idea. You might use work retirement plans; IRAs (Individual Retirement Accounts); business-owner plans like SEP-IRAs, SIMPLE IRAs and "solo" 401Ks; tax-exempt municipal bonds and bond funds; low-cost annuities; low- or no-dividend stocks; tax-efficient mutual funds; and index funds are all tax-smart options.

9. Not Having Enough Life Insurance

If you have no heirs or charities to leave money to then you probably don't need much life insurance. If you have loved ones, seriously consider the right amount of coverage. There are many methods to figure this. The easiest way is to visit a website like *SmartMoney.com* (look under "tools" then "insurance"). Input your information and coverage is estimated for your situation.

10. Relying on Only One Opinion

If a doctor told you it was necessary to get invasive surgery, you might be inclined to get another opinion. In the same way, if a professional advisor gives you a recommendation, you should consider a second viewpoint. Although not as important as our health, our wealth definitely deserves the thought of more than one advisor. Ask each one you visit with some of the questions mentioned in part one. Compare their answers and get an idea of which person best fits your goals and investment attitude.

* * *

"Retirement at sixty-five is ridiculous. When I was sixty-five I still had pimples."

—George Burns

Originally published in December, 2011.

QUOTES

> "You can beat the market by ignoring the herd."
>
> —Peter Lynch

> "A decline is a great opportunity to pick up bargains left behind by investors who are fleeing the storm in panic."
>
> —Peter Lynch

> "The time of maximum pessimism is the best time to buy. The time of maximum optimism is the best time to sell."
>
> —Sir John Templeton

> "Risk is not knowing what you're doing."
>
> —Warren Buffett

> "All investors do is learn how to have their money work hard for them."
>
> —Robert Kiyosaki

> "Holders of stocks...have the possibility that a loss of the dollar's purchasing power may be offset by advances in their dividends and the prices of their shares."
>
> —Benjamin Graham

> "I never lost money by turning a profit."
>
> —Bernard Baruch

> "It is well enough that people of the nation do not understand our banking and monetary system, for if they did, I believe there would be a revolution before tomorrow morning."
>
> —Henry Ford

> "Many of the biggest and most far-reaching investments we make in our lives are investments that have little or nothing to do with money."
>
> —Daniel Quinn

> "The safe way to double your money is to fold it over once and put it in your pocket."
>
> —Frank Hubbard

> "A steady job and a mutual fund is still the best defense against social security."
>
> —Author Unknown

> "My problem lies in reconciling my gross habits with my net income."
>
> —Errol Flynn

> "An investor without investment objectives is like a traveler without a destination."
>
> —Ralph Seger

> "Only buy something that you'd be perfectly happy to hold if the market shut down for ten years."
>
> —Warren Buffett

> "It is not from the benevolence of the butcher, the brewer, or the baker that we expect our dinner, but from their regard to their own interest."
>
> —Adam Smith

"What material success does is provide you with the ability to concentrate on other things that really matter. And that is being able to make a difference, not only in your own life, but in other people's lives."

—Oprah Winfrey

"Economic development over the past two centuries has taken most of humanity...to personal health and security, material comfort and knowledge that were unknown to the elites of the wealthiest and most powerful societies in earlier times."

—Ross Garnaut

"Money is like manure. You have to spread it around or it smells."

—J. Paul Getty

--ABOUT THE AUTHOR--

Ronald Phillips was born and raised in Pueblo, Colorado. He graduated from Central High School and attended, what was then, the University of Southern Colorado. He has been advising clients on their investments since the year 2000. He currently manages several million dollars in assets for dozens of clients throughout the United States.

THE AUTHOR CAN BE CONTACTED AT:

311 West 24th Street, Suite 4
Pueblo, CO 81003

(719) 545-6442
RonPhillipsAdvisor@gmail.com

The Most Implausible
<u>FREE</u> Gift Ever

($527.88 Worth of Financial Planning)

Ron Phillips, Independent Financial Advisor, is willing to give away a heap of freebies that are <u>like having a licensed advisor in a box</u>. This is an unprecedented offer. Most <u>advisors</u> (or brokers, planners, etc) either <u>don't give this information out OR they charge $1,000s and $1,000s in fees</u> for this instructional info. You'll receive an avalanche of exclusive guidance, including:

Professionally Prepared Financial Mini-Plan (Value = $475)
* Retirement Plan Spend Down Worksheet
* Financial Foundations Info Sheet
* <u>Your Personalized</u> Asset Allocation Plan
* Net Worth Statement…and more

REPORT: Create Your Own Lifetime Pension (Value = $14.97)
* Create Lifetime, Pension-Like income
* Guaranteed Income Growth
* Guaranteed Account Value Growth
* Professional Asset Allocation Creation and Re-Balancing Secrets

REPORT: Create a "Dynamic Income Portfolio" (Value = $14.97)
* Learn Benjamin Graham's (Warren Buffetts' mentor) Secret Strategy
* Prepare for Inflation, Deflation, Recessions, Taxes and more
* Create Income Now AND Leave Money for Your Loved Ones
* Learn the Secrets of <u>True</u> Diversification and the Power of Investing Hedges

AUDIO CD: The 10 Most-Tragic Investor Mistakes (Value = 22.94)
* Avoid the Least-Understood, <u>Most-Abused</u> Investment on the Market
* Learn the Right Questions to Ask Before Hiring a Financial Advisor
* The One Thing <u>Not</u> to Rely on When Investing

TWO WAYS TO GET THE "ADVISOR IN A BOX"

(1) Visit: RetireIQ.com
(2) Call and leave a message: **719-924-5070**

REMEMBER: <u>Please mention Promo Code #9002 when ordering</u>

RON'S FIRST BOOK HAS HELPED HUNDREDS OF INVESTORS LIKE YOU

FROM TRUSTED and INDEPENDENT financial advisor, Ron Phillips, comes one of the most concise investment books written. It will help answer many investment questions that you were unsure of asking your stockbroker or other advisors.

INVESTING TO WIN is filled with valuable information such as:

- The hidden fee structure of the four most-common mutual funds
- Differences between "open-end" and "closed-end" mutual funds and why one might be better than the other
- Valuable strategies to give you an edge such as: Ron's proprietary FDCF Strategy© , Dollar-Cost Averaging, The 3-Step No-Brainer Mutual Fund Strategy among others
- The ins and outs of annuities
- How to create tax-exempt income AND MORE...

Buy at **amazon**.com—just search "Ron Phillips investing"

Made in the USA
Columbia, SC
10 July 2019